William Walter Bode

Lights and Shadows of Chinatown

William Walter Bode

Lights and Shadows of Chinatown

ISBN/EAN: 9783743333994

Manufactured in Europe, USA, Canada, Australia, Japa

Cover: Foto ©ninafisch / pixelio.de

Manufactured and distributed by brebook publishing software
(www.brebook.com)

William Walter Bode

Lights and Shadows of Chinatown

Old Saint Mary's Cathedral, with Green Cadog Tower in the distance.

(The Gate-way, so to speak, to Cape Town.)

perhaps it is not possible, wholly to realize, as we drift along the busy stream of Oriental life, that we have not been translated to a strange land. Buildings have been evolved, and others shaped out of semblance to their original design, wherever and whenever possible, with pagan architecture and imagery. It is here and there only that portions of solid masonry remain which have defied the sons of Confucius to mar; and some solemn griffin, or gargoyle carving, is yet imbedded beneath cornice, or gracing some Corinthian colonnade, as if looking down in apparent sadness at its own strange environment, reminding us that but a comparatively brief period has elapsed since dwelt here those hardy pioneers whose bending forms are only occasionally seen visiting the old haunts, rich in pathetic and tragical episodes and heroic deeds of a half century ago.

Here the visitor is apt to regard the encroachment which the Chinese have made on the acreage of this section of the city as an interesting phenomenon, from a single primitive "wash-house," erected as a necessity on Portsmouth Square, now known as the Plaza, until this quarter now comprises over fifteen blocks of houses, wholly within the city limits, and wherein, as near as can be computed, about fifty thousand Chinese reside and do business, and, like the glacier of the north, still spreads and moves on. Fortunately, the salt ocean

Fireplace & Archway – At Chinese Mission

Panel over Fireplace at Chinese Mission

"THUMB-NAIL" SKETCHES.

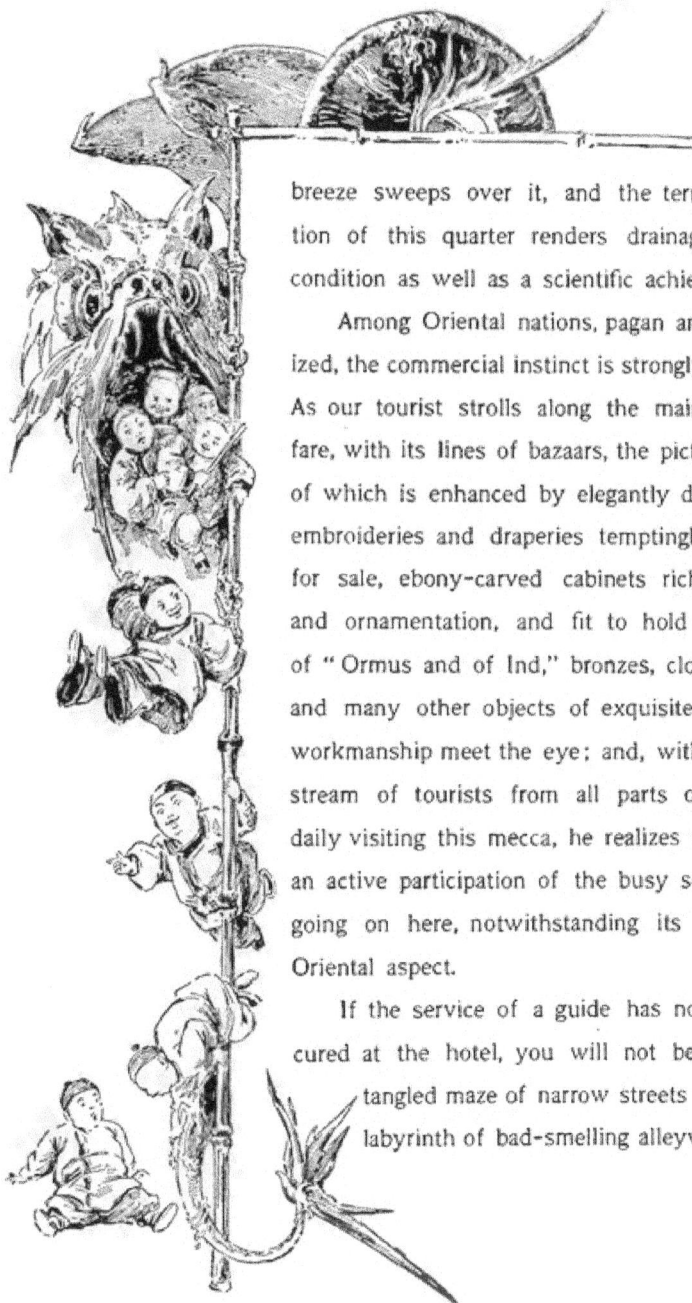

breeze sweeps over it, and the terraced condition of this quarter renders drainage a natural condition as well as a scientific achievement.

Among Oriental nations, pagan and christianized, the commercial instinct is strongly developed. As our tourist strolls along the main thoroughfare, with its lines of bazaars, the picturesqueness of which is enhanced by elegantly decorated silk embroideries and draperies temptingly displayed for sale, ebony-carved cabinets rich in design and ornamentation, and fit to hold the wealth of "Ormus and of Ind," bronzes, cloisonne ware and many other objects of exquisite beauty and workmanship meet the eye; and, with a constant stream of tourists from all parts of the world daily visiting this mecca, he realizes that there is an active participation of the busy scenes of life going on here, notwithstanding its antique and Oriental aspect.

If the service of a guide has not been procured at the hotel, you will not be lost in the tangled maze of narrow streets and dubious labyrinth of bad-smelling alleyways, for the denizens of this quarter thoroughly appreciate the desire which prevails to penetrate and investigate the inner life of their people. Solicitations are made, at every crossing, to guide and conduct you to the various shrines and objects of curiosity which abound here ; they seem to alight on the pilgrim intuitively, and vie with each other in an exaggeration of promises rarely fulfilled. It is delightful to watch the tactics of these subtle fellows,—the ingenious harangue, their skill in unmasking the stranger, their epigrammatic rendition of the sights to be seen. They learn each other's tricks and the usual line of approach in dealing with a "tenderfoot" or European tourist. A wily looking fellow approached us one evening, and, after delivering the usual prelude to excite our curiosity, actually showed us a glimpse of his return certificate, issued by the powers that be at the Custom House, and, with a suavity and blandness of manner really amusing, assured us that it was a special license granted to ply his vocation as guide, for services rendered to the Government. "All Melica man know Charlie ; heep good guide ! Twenty-six years Chinatown !" It is perhaps superfluous to state that, with ew exceptions, they are adept in all guileful arts, crafty, knavish and suspicious.

Stroll where you will you meet on every side evidences of another and departed regime, and find curious studies, many of

"ON THE LOOKOUT."
(Where the Deadly Highbinder Holds Forth.)

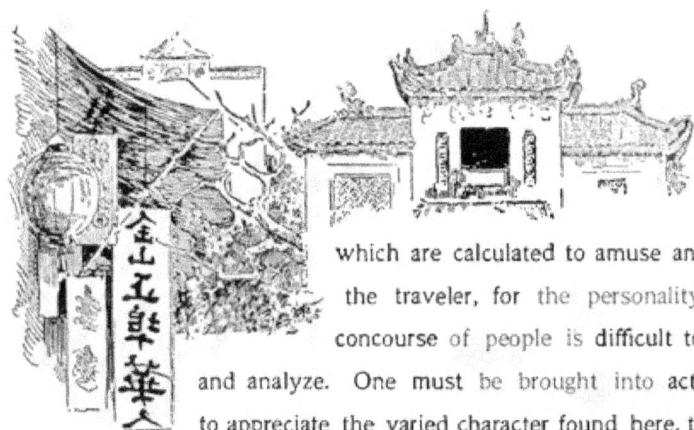

which are calculated to amuse and instruct the traveler, for the personality of this concourse of people is difficult to describe and analyze. One must be brought into actual touch to appreciate the varied character found here, the variety of things to admire and to wonder at, others to ponder over, and all of them interesting. It does not seem possible that you can stroll block after block without encountering a single Christian place of business in this quarter, yet so it is. You will wonder how and why there has been such a transfiguration in this heritage; you will realize, however, by the compass of your stroll, that you are obtaining a visit to China without being obliged to cross the Pacific, or wrestle with that much-dreaded monster, seasickness. You will investigate narrow, serpentine passages under ground and above ground, to unfathom which it will be necessary to have an experienced and trustworthy guide; you will review scores of opium joints beneath stained and cobwebbed frescoes, and hear the click of the domino in the game of pi-gou as you pass the broad but scarred and battered portal of what was once some stately dwelling; you will meet at intervals athletic looking officials in disguise, reconnoitering up some dark, foul-smelling, tortuous passage, or escalading some perilous roof to cut off the retreat from a game of fan tan, or sup choy, in full blast in the vicinity, and the approach to which is guarded by an array of formidable barriers and sesames, as only the cunning Chinese can develop or their ingenuity create.

At a prominent corner near the farther end of the main thoroughfare, you will find a building, the history of which dates back half a century ago, now a ruined pile of weather-beaten brick.   Neither its interior nor exterior has felt the touch of brush or trowel for many, many years.   The work of subjugation has been done, and this ancient, crumbling, interesting landmark known as the Globe Hotel now shelters the flotsam and jetsam of Chinatown.   Everything is steeped to the lips in the spirit of paganism, and by its exterior only do we recognize the features and individualities of days dead and gone. Its four stories lift up, row upon row of carved and highly elaborated pediments; and from its upper windows the belfric towers of St. Francis of Assissium, and the spires of Senora de Guadaloupe, at the northern extremity of this quarter, are plainly visible, whilst Mount Tamalpais may be viewed across the Bay in a warp of woven sunshine, guarding, sentinel-like, the approach to the entrance of the Golden Gate, and sheltering the flower

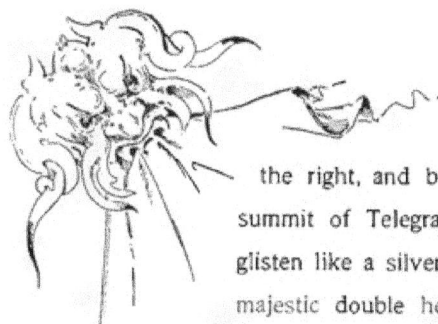

decked homes of Sausalito and San Rafael; and farther away to the right, and beneath the deserted citadel at the summit of Telegraph Hill, the Straits of Carquinez glisten like a silver bar in the morning light; and the majestic double head of Mount Diablo lifts in hazy distance from the purple maze and tender tints which embosom the lovely stretch of landscape called the Ignacio Valley; and in the history of this once important structure is found the record of feud and strife, love and romance, of the ever-shifting scenes enacted in

" The days of old,
The days of gold,
The days of 'Forty-nine.''

Not less interesting, and not far from this corner, is a ruined portal, conspicuous in the fact that here resided Madam Ah Toy, the first Chinese woman to grace these shores with her presence. She was evidently a lady of wealth and high caste, of rare attainments, simple sincerity, and of intellect keen and discriminating, gifted with uncommon foresight, and at whose receptions and levees the ecclesiastical and political savant of the hour would meet, and at whose tea parties it was considered a rare privilege and honor to be invited. It was her influence that prompted the then resident Chinese to accept the invitation

·

to actively participate in the ceremonies, held with such eclat, to commemorate the admission of California into the Union, in 1850. This must be regarded as particularly noteworthy. The thinness of population and smallness of trade at that time, allied to the isolated locality of San Francisco, rendered every effort to open up foreign trade a desideratum; and many propositions were entertained that would lead to more extended commercial relations with the Orient; so it was especially by our own solicitation that we have now safely harbored here the active, competing foreign element which has created so much discussion and argument on the political horizon, and upon whom it has been considered necessary for our well-being to levy the Restriction Act, now so called.

I had always a desire to visit this spot, and shall never forget my first impression of this quarter. It has been my privilege since then to visit it again and again,—I might say, almost to reside there; and, in the light of what has been revealed to me through many later observations, I consider it was a rare opportunity that permitted the witnessing of a spectacle which no subsequent picture has approached, either in color or arrangement.

It was in February, and the rain which had been deluging the land had abated near midnight. The Feast of Lanterns was

CHINESE JOSS HOUSE.
(Afternoon.)

THE HOUSING OF A PAGAN GOD

on the programme, and the housing
of the Pagan Deities, a ceremony
of rare occurrence, was to be con-
summated that evening. It was with the expec-
tation of seeing something new and strange
in aspect that induced me to wend my way
through the damp and deserted avenues of
approach, while dark, lowering rainclouds threat-
ened ominously overhead. We ascended the
tower of old St. Mary's Cathedral, situated at
the first terrace-rising, and from its summit
the mellow tint which welled up against the black, starless
background melted away in the tremulous wide scene of
ten thousand more of decorated, lighted lanterns, strung in
graceful abandon from column portal and balcony, down the
gradual incline, and as slowly rising again until the farther
extremity of this undulating perspective was reached, terrace
upon terrace lifted out from this central line, illuminating in
turn myriads of window gardens, gilded oriels and arabesque
balconies. The undulating character of the land lent additional
beauty to this fairy-like panorama. I could hardly restrain my
delight; it was so unlike anything I had ever seen before.
Whilst enjoying this midnight feast there slowly entered upon

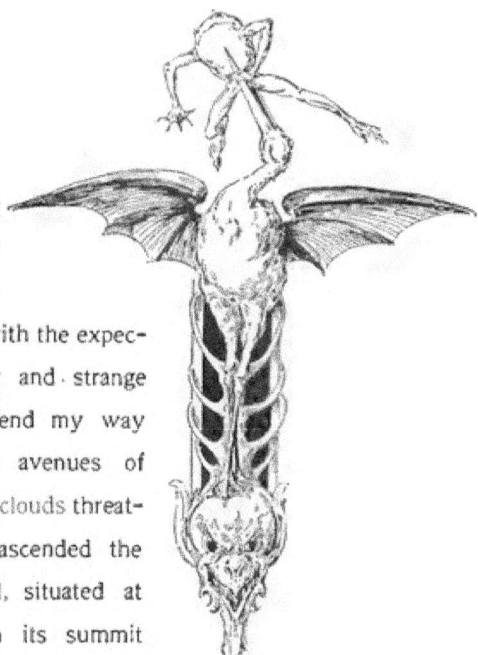

the main avenue a procession heralded by an orchestra of clashing cymbals, unmusical tom-toms, and gaily decked fiddlers, followed by a retinue of priests in long, showy silken robes and bright vestments, who alternately chanted, with peculiar intonation and inflation, mystic "canzoni" or sacred lays, which tradition tells us were sung two thousand years before the christian era. The aristocracy of wealth were there in royal habiliments, each representative carrying frames of burning punks and brass talismans; and high upon a gorgeous, sculptured throne, which was borne by forty or more men in fantastic garb, sat in stoic indifference, beneath flaunting dragons, the divinities of the heathen pantheon, amid a wealth of tinsel and elaborate gildings.

This procession came up the main thoroughfare, and, as it traversed again and became lost to view, it seemed from my dizzy height more like a dreamy symphonic arrangement of color than the actual presentment of an Oriental ceremony enacted within the framing of these historic precincts.

We now enter a short street rich in reminiscences; here the first residence was built; and we immediately come to a charming study of a dwelling with a corinthian colonnade supporting a balcony of odd design in rich translucent green, peculiarly Chinese. It is unusually well preserved for this quarter, and

CHINESE ROOF-HOUSES

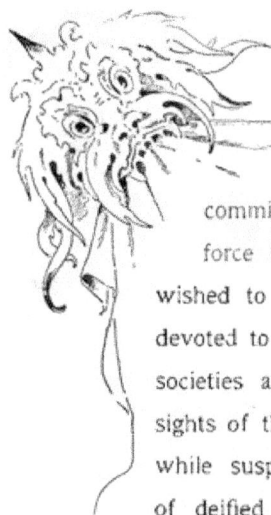

is pointed out as once the residence of a prominent member of the vigilance committee which operated here with such crushing force in the suppression of the lawless bandits who wished to overthrow rule and order in 1856. It is now devoted to the use of one of the many Chinese benevolent societies as a pantheon, and is regarded as one of the sights of this quarter. Its upper floors enshrine the Gods, while suspended in boxes along the corridors are numbers of deified warriors, heroes and sages, in attitudes as if trampling victorious over some prostrate foe ; while concealed springs cause them automatically to flourish javelins and other warlike weapons of cruel design. Semi-annual banquets are served here to the promoters of the association, and on these occasions, from an improvised niche, the usual orchestra accompany from midday until midnight a sort of recitative, relieved at intervals with a sforzando movement that creates din sufficient to raise the firmament ; while the admiring canaille read from large paper curtains of deep vermilion dye, hanging outside, the names of the contributors and their respective donations to this association, and of the evil spirits that have been controlled under their incantations and exorcisms. The terrifying effigies of two of these devils are placed on high and exposed to view, and made to face the rising sun every morning during ceremonial week. When adequate expiation has been made, and they have been sufficiently rebuked- in this novel manner, by comparison to the orb of day, they are forcibly projected at midnight from the balcony above to the street pavement, where the exorcist or devil-killer works for several hours, with numerous curses, written in red ink upon yellow paper, which he then burns on a porcelain plate, and the ashes stirred into a cup of water. With his mouth filled with this holy water, a trident in one hand, and in the other an engraved bit of wood, weighty with virtue for the overthrow of these demons that vex the good Chinaman's peace and happiness, he stamps around, thrusting and brandishing his trident, holding aloft his magic wand, spurting water from his mouth in every direction, commanding the devils in his loudest voice to depart, yelling and howling until the first streak of light breaks the horizon, when these effigies are incinerated with additional hubbub and their ashes scattered from brazen vessels to the morning breeze.

Each succeeding decade has given this street additional history. It was originally called Calle de las Rosas, in honor of its many rose-covered cottages. From here the pioneers viewed with delight the illumined tips of Telegraph and Russian hills, which augured the sighting of some expected ship that

W. Bode

would bring them again in touch with distant hearts after many months of weary and anxious waiting; for the waters yet ebbed and flowed at Montgomery Street, and the deep golden eschscholtzia, nature's floral beacon and emblem of the illimitable wealth in this el dorado, was not yet shorn nor ruthlessly riven from its native bed in the sand dunes above in the rush for greed and gain which subsequently followed.

A decade later and these delightful and cherished homes were subjected to a transformation: a reign of the demi-monde was inaugurated, and the name of Pike Street was substituted for the euphonious Calle de las Rosas. Under this baneful regime its notoriety soon echoed to the base of the Rockies. There are associated with this era many sensational episodes of good deeds and heinous crimes. Particularly characteristic and worthy of repetition is that story where the "soul of goodness is mixed with things evil," and which has but recently reached its final tableau, after the curtain had been rung down and the dramatis personæ had left the stage of action five and thirty years ago. It is told that the young and beautiful daughter of a wealthy Parisian, who had loved, "not wisely, but too well," and had to flee the paternal

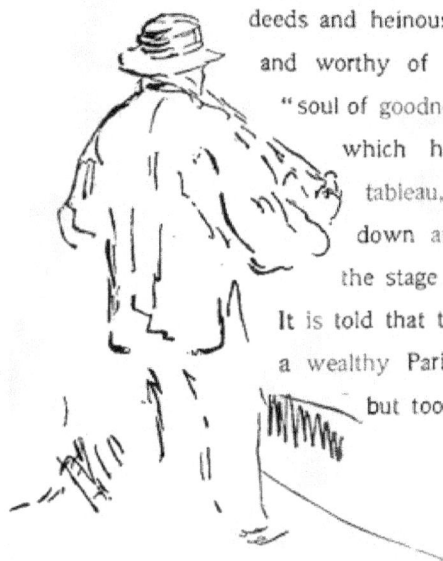

wrath, made her advent in 'Frisco when the gold fever was at its zenith. Her youth, extraordinary beauty and dashing style created much admiration, and, being a person in fine, with natural and acquired tastes and propensities, she readily obtained an *entrée* into the best society of that day. With a charm of manner rivaled only by the accomplishments of her mind, she successfully essayed the role of an adventuress, and by her wily intrigues soon amassed a small fortune. Her true character being revealed, she was soon forsaken, and drifted to this street, where she plunged into a career of reckless abandon.

The finding of her body in the ransacked boudoir of her dwelling, with the imprint of a brawny hand upon her delicate neck, plainly told its story, and was the sensation of the day. Her male associate was held, and the evidence, although purely circumstantial, seemed incriminatory, when another deed, similarly perpetrated, for the same purpose and upon a like character, was discovered in the valley of the Sacramento River.

No direct clue was unearthed to either of these atrocities until, at one of those Bohemian socials so prevalent in that early day, there was lost, and found, a diamond bracelet, on the reverse side of which was chased this inscription:

A notre fille,
Marie Banier.

It was a souvenir from the parents of the unfortunate Parisienne on attaining her majority; it was returned to the claimant, a lady, who little dreamt that in establishing her right to this cluster of diamonds she had unconsciously raised the curtain upon the participants of this drama, and exposed to view the perpetrator of both of these crimes, and who was none other than her own husband. The arrested consort of the Parisienne was released and soon after reached Paris, where he succeeded in obtaining possession of, and lived in fine style upon, the income of his dead mistress' property, to the exclusion of the child she had left behind, and for whose education and welfare she had sacrificed her honor and very life.

During all this time San Francisco was undergoing its wonderful transformation: the city was spreading beyond the hills; the old-fashioned little cottages, and the mountain goats that browsed around the flinty heights of Nob Hill, were disturbed by the advent of the cable car; magnificent and palatial mansions were being erected thereon, and what was at one time a fashionable center soon became the habitation of the incoming Mongolians. With this third transformation came the name of Waverly Place. The gay characters who had flitted here for over a decade sought other pastures, and the Chinese took possession of the street. With the date of their advent we enter upon the second part of this sensational drama.

Under the shadows of two cathedrals, Grace and St. Mary's, stood the cottage where the unfortunate Parisienne dwelt. It had now passed into the possession of the Chinese, who felt that the time was opportune for the erection of a pagan temple that would vie with its stately christian sisters, gracefully and strikingly imposed upon the terrace beyond.

In the removal of this cottage was unearthed a box containing title deeds to valuable property in Paris from Marie Banier to her son, Perrier Banier, and a certificate of deposit for a princely sum of money in bank. This information soon reached Paris, where it was learned that the legacy of her early love had now grown to man's estate. By the accidental discovery of these papers he was enabled to receive this long buried and now resurrected tribute of maternal devotion.

Further along this street, just at the corner, there has been erected a small Protestant church, to do battle, as it were, with the number of divinities of the heathen Pantheon ensconced along the line, a Lilliput among the Brobdinags. A few Chinese

A VIEW OF BARTLETT ALLEY.

FISH-MARKET MEMORANDA.

under its influence have dared to emancipate themselves from conventional mannerisms, and enthusiastically seek proselytes even at the very doors of the sanctuaries where the orthodox Chinese worship. No one but a person who has lived in China can form any idea of the hindrances in the way of christianizing the native residents. Three things are responsible for this, says a recent convert, "the worshiping of ancestors of idols, and the fear of the Chinese that the Christians wish to destroy the native customs and traditions, and eventually enthrall them." Filial reverence and obedience are characteristic traits of the Chinese. These sentiments extend beyond the grave; so that, when parents die, prayers are addressed to them as guardian spirits. By them the subordination of individual rights to those of the family is regarded as a fundamental and irrevocable principle; hence every Chinaman, in forsaking paganism, must obtain the consent of his family if he wishes assurance from future proscription. Every divinity is endowed with certain characteristics, and the embodiment of some special function or attribute of humanity, the unvarying belief in the existence and personality of their deities, upon whose active agency their votaries rely, is, without doubt, the underlying principle of their superstition.

The Chinaman is a great believer in spirits, particularly those with an evil disposition. His upper world is peopled by Gods and his under world by multitudes of devils. Incense is freely burned before the household shrine, and fervent and divers prayers are continually offered to rid their houses of these unwelcome visitors.

Among the peculiar features of paganism there is none more revolting than the cruelty practiced upon young girls, based upon a system of slavery. It is a prolific source of corruption and degradation, and has had much license in this quarter.

The profound pity felt for these unhappy victims, who, from ignorance, adverse conditions of heredity and environment, are being continually bought and sold, smuggled on steamers or over the boundary lines, has awakened an effort to abridge, if not actually suppress, this traffic, which prevails in all the heartless cruelty which characterized that condition at the close of the Roman Republic.

By the untiring and zealous efforts of a missionary lady, who has devoted nearly a score of years to ameliorating the condition of her sex, there have been rescued from brothels five hundred or more Chinese girls, whose ages range from nine to fifteen years, and the purchase price of whom aggregated over a

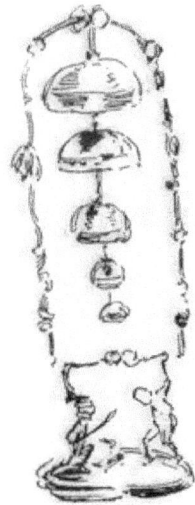

million dollars. They have been comfortably housed, their religious instruction fostered, their physical condition toned, and every possible effort enlisted to lift them up to a sphere of honor and usefulness. By the aid of these simple elements, the employment of time, with a certain customary and moral discipline controlled by kindness, a great work has been done, and many of them are now the happy wives and mothers of pleasant homes.

The law in regard to this slave traffic is specific and exacting; but there is a spirit prevalent in this neighborhood which the French call "*l'esprit de localité*," which often warps the judgment of the most upright and honest men, and when, by the assistance of legal technicalities, this spirit is coupled to a writ of *habeas corpus* procedure, to be subsequently investigated by the Federal courts, the law becomes elastic, and the victim is permitted to land, to be as readily delivered to some execrable hag of moral unconsciousness and indifference of feeling, of insolent manners

and savage temper, for a moneyed consideration varying from five hundred to four thousand dollars, according to the girl's age and personal attraction.

Should the child be one of tender years, she is now made to perform menial drudgery, and is frequently treated not only unkindly, but cruelly. At maturity the slave girl becomes more valuable. Here for a time she is kept under strict surveillance; her avocation and environment leave no opportunity for intellectual effort. She is bedecked with gaudy trinkets, zealously guarded, and now begins a slavery of many years and of a fiercer kind. Her mind generally is dethroned under her former treatment, and she generally subserves the will of her owner. The best part of her life is wasted amidst unfriendly and degraded companions: she finds no comfort in life, nothing to love, nothing to hope for; family and friends are to her as though they were not, and very few, if any, have any recollection whatever of parents or relations.

It is not indeed strange, when the door is closed and the key turned on these deluded creatures in a strange land, that they occasionally awake from their terror to a realism of the condition which deprives them of bodily and mental freedom, and attempt to break from this bondage and flee at the peril of their lives to the refuge home provided for them by a kind and humane association.

A CHINESE MERCHANT

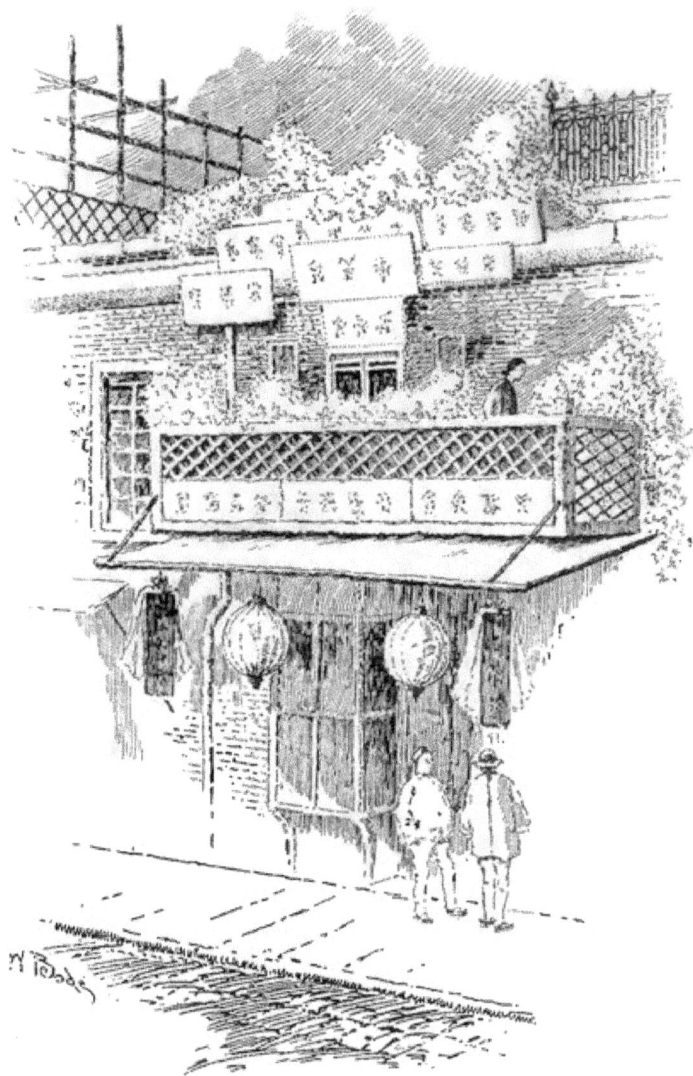

Whenever it becomes known that there is a girl of legal age thus environed, efforts are made to ascertain the opinion she entertains as to the desirability of her removal. It is known that, in their powerless and helpless condition, so much insincerity has been forced upon them, and such frightful pictures presented to their ignorant minds of the brutalities and enslavement practiced by Christians, that it becomes necessary to free her mind from these prejudices, as initiatory measures to a successful rescue. A careful diagram of the building is made, and every known avenue of escape guarded, when a raid is attempted, and the rescue party, under police surveillance, ultimately removes the trembling victim from her surroundings, amid a crowd of infuriated "high-binders," human hyenas, whose fierce anathemas and savage threats fill the air. Frequently, however, notwithstanding all of these carefully planned measures, the victim is quickly spirited away through some secret trap or panel leading into an underground or overhead network of passages, to be again secreted until the rescue is abandoned or given up in despair.

There is something of interest to be learned in every square foot of these old precincts. For years I thought I knew all that there was to know about this quarter, but every additional

tour of inspection reveals some new interest; and the traveler who simply pays a flying visit here has only sipped, *not drunk*, at this fountain. He must explore for himself the various regions of interest, which will open to him a boundless source of wonder and study; for in this, one of the finest parts of the town, and the oldest district, occupying, I may say almost profaning, in many respects, its once stately homes, is deeply intrenched and emphasized a condition of society and civilization of which its adaptability to circumstances is our marvel, and the fruit of thousands of years of abnegation and Oriental estrangement.

There are no words wherein to describe, no measure wherewith to measure, the subtleties and eccentricities which, living constantly in a thickly settled section like this, and among these people, is apt to generate, where so many people are crowded into so little room, where the aggregate of suffering must be multiplied by every individual tale of woe; yet how unlike the east side of New York, the tenement districts of London or of Paris. The traveler here can go where he listeth, and at whatever hour he pleaseth. He is not disturbed by beggars nor by drunken brawls; nor is he liable to the dangers which bestrew his path among Christians in either of the places mentioned. He is free from molestation, ridicule

A CHINA TOWN BALCONY.

and banter; and, from all that we have seen, he will find on the whole a personally clean, sober, sagacious and industrious people. "No! Let this section be as wicked and as malodorous as the reports make it to be; let the viscious be as thick and the taste for the meretricious and artificial be as apparently uppermost: the lovers of goodness are many; the supporters and seekers for what is pure and right are the substantial bulk of these people."

WILLIAM WALTER BODE.

PROCESSION OF "WONG FONG" (THE DRAGON).

www.ingramcontent.com/pod-product-compliance
Lightning Source LLC
Chambersburg PA
CBHW020235090426
42735CB00010B/1710